Eye Wonder

Rocks
and
Minerals

LONDON, NEW YORK, MUNICH,
MELBOURNE, and DELHI

Written and edited by Caroline Bingham
Designed by Helen Chapman
Publishing manager Susan Leonard
Managing art editor Clare Shedden
Jacket design Chris Drew
Picture researcher Sarah Stewart-Richardson
Production Shivani Pandey
DTP Designer Almudena Díaz
Consultant Kim Dennis-Bryan PhD, FZS
With thanks to Victoria Long
for design assistance.

First American Edition, 2004
Published in the United States by
DK Publishing, Inc., 375 Hudson Street,
New York, New York 10014

10 15 14 13

Library of Congress Cataloging-in-Publication Data
Bingham, Caroline, 1962-
Rocks and minerals / by Caroline Bingham.-- 1st American ed.
p. cm. -- (Eye wonder)
Includes bibliographical references and index.
Contents: Rocky earth -- Volcanic beginnings -- Making of a
rock -- Igneous rock -- Sedimentary rock -- Metamorphic rock -
- Rocks from space -- Hidden beauty -- Breakdown -- Carving
a path -- What is a crystal? -- What a gem! -- Mineral
treasures -- Are metals rocks? -- Rocks and their uses --
Minerals, minerals everywhere -- A touch of mystery -- History
in a rock -- Digging up dinosaurs -- The bigger picture --
Mineral alphabet.
ISBN 978-0-7894-9894-6 (ALB) -- ISBN 978-0-7894-9760-4
1. Minerals--Juvenile literature. 2. Rocks--Juvenile literature.
[1. Minerals. 2. Rocks.] I. Title. II. Series.
QE365.2.B56 2004
549--dc22
2003016048

Color reproduction by Colourscan, Singapore
Printed and bound in Italy by L.E.G.O.

discover more at
www.dk.com

Contents

car

telephone

jewelry

clothes

Rocky Earth

Rocks and minerals are important. They make up much of our planet and are mined to provide many of the things around us, from cars to computers. Even your body contains minerals that keep you alive.

toothpaste

computer

house

you and me!

quartz crystals + feldspar crystals + mica crystals = granite (a type of rock)

Feldspar (pink and white)

Mica (black)

Quartz (gray)

Let's make a rock

Rocks are made up of crystals of minerals. Different amounts of minerals make up different rocks (though some rocks are made from just one mineral).

Earth's crust is between 3 ½ and 42 miles (5 and 68 km) thick.

Most of the crust and mantle is made from lots of different rocks, all squashed together.

Earth's crust

Mantle

Outer core

Core

Scientists believe Earth was born about 4,6 billion years ago.

Store cupboard

The things we use in our everyday lives come from our planet, Earth. The raw ingredients are all taken from the crust. We cannot drill any deeper.

Mineral facts

- Your body contains more than 60 minerals. Nine of these are essential for life.

- Some minerals take thousands of years to form. Some form in minutes.

Let's make shampoo

What forms the shampoo you use on your hair? Minerals, including those below!

coal tar + lithium clay + selenium = shampoo

A volcanic beginning

Squeeze clay in your hands and it oozes between your fingers. This is a little like what happens inside a volcano. The pressure grows until the volcano erupts. Whoosh! It is the first step in the formation of new rocks.

When magma leaves a volcano, it is called lava.

The magma is forced up inside the volcano.

Previous eruptions have formed a cone-shaped exterior.

Magma (molten rock) chamber.

No place for a rock?

Deep, deep under Earth's crust, it is hot enough to melt rock. This molten rock sometimes builds up in chambers and bursts through weak spots in Earth's crust.

Avalanche of rock

A volcano erupts with such power that sometimes the eruption destroys a part of the volcano. Huge rocks shoot into the air.

Volcanic debris ranges from dust and ash to rocks the size of houses.

Just a cliff?

The eruption of a volcano can create deep layers of ash, dust, and rock at its base. It changes the landscape.

Shiprock

Shiprock Pinnacle is all that remains of an ancient volcano. It is the hardened core.

Shiprock Pinnacle is named after a ship, as it looks a little like one.

Shiprock Pinnacle in New Mexico was once a plug of magma filling the chimney vent of a volcano.

Making of a rock

Do you think that all rocks look the same? In fact, there are many different kinds of rocks, but they can be divided into three basic types, which are being formed (and destroyed) as you read this book.

In the beginning

Earth's first rocks were igneous rocks. These form from molten rock that has cooled and hardened.

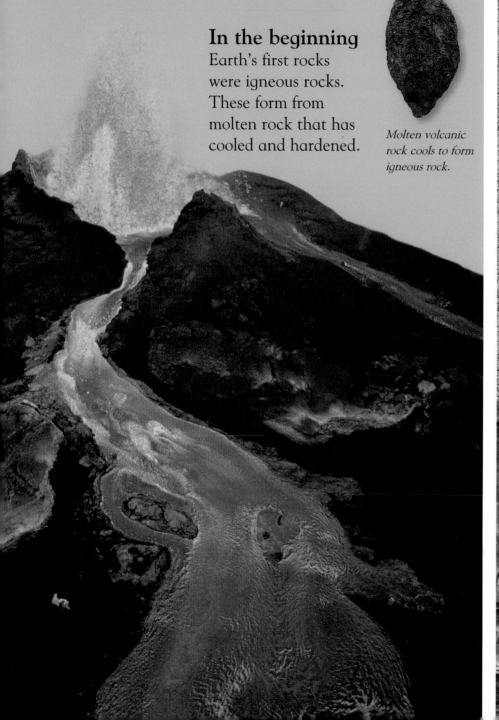

Molten volcanic rock cools to form igneous rock.

Chipping away

One way sedimentary rock forms is when pieces of rock are carried to the sea, where they create huge piles of sediment. After thousands of years these cement together.

Sedimentary rock

Sediments are

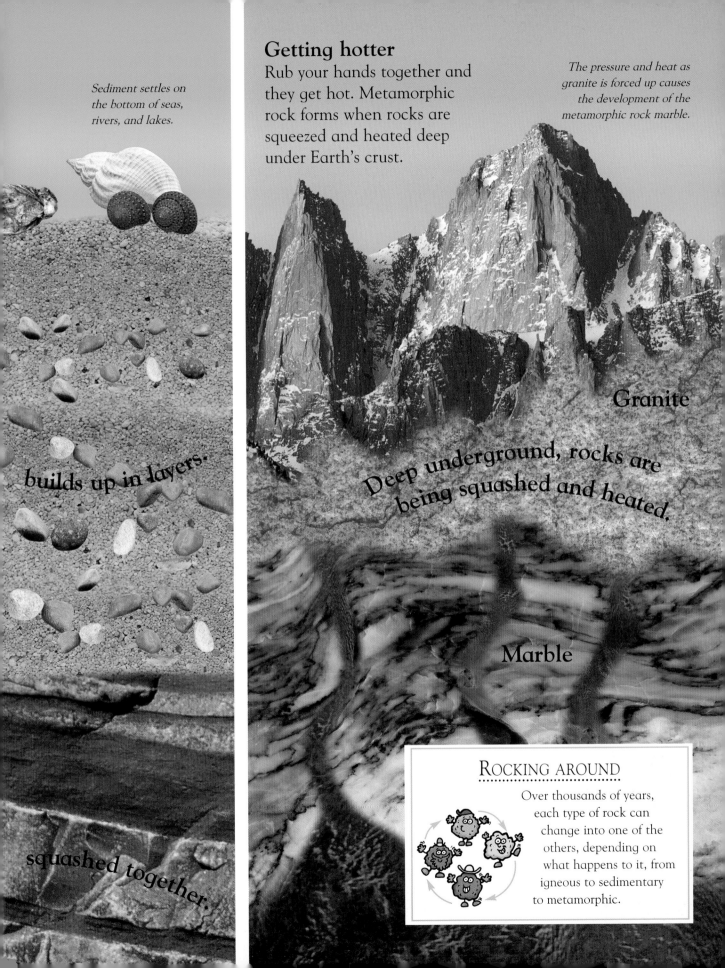

Sediment settles on the bottom of seas, rivers, and lakes.

builds up in layers.

squashed together.

Getting hotter

Rub your hands together and they get hot. Metamorphic rock forms when rocks are squeezed and heated deep under Earth's crust.

The pressure and heat as granite is forced up causes the development of the metamorphic rock marble.

Granite

Deep underground, rocks are being squashed and heated.

Marble

ROCKING AROUND

Over thousands of years, each type of rock can change into one of the others, depending on what happens to it, from igneous to sedimentary to metamorphic.

Igneous rock

Igneous rocks form the greatest part of Earth's rocky crust, but can also be seen in the land around us. A famous igneous rock landscape is the Giant's Causeway in Northern Ireland.

Pele's hair looks like hair! It forms from sprays of lava.

Pumice stone is the only floating rock.

Obsidian has a shiny surface. It contains a lot of glass.

Pumice is an igneous rock from the heart of a volcano.

From hair to glass
A volcano produces a great variety of igneous rocks. Just take a look at the three examples shown above.

London's Tower Bridge uses granite.

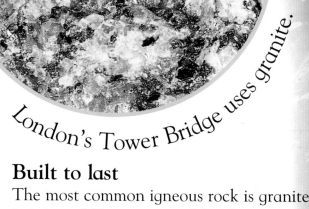

Built to last
The most common igneous rock is granite. It is incredibly strong, and has been used for building for thousands of years.

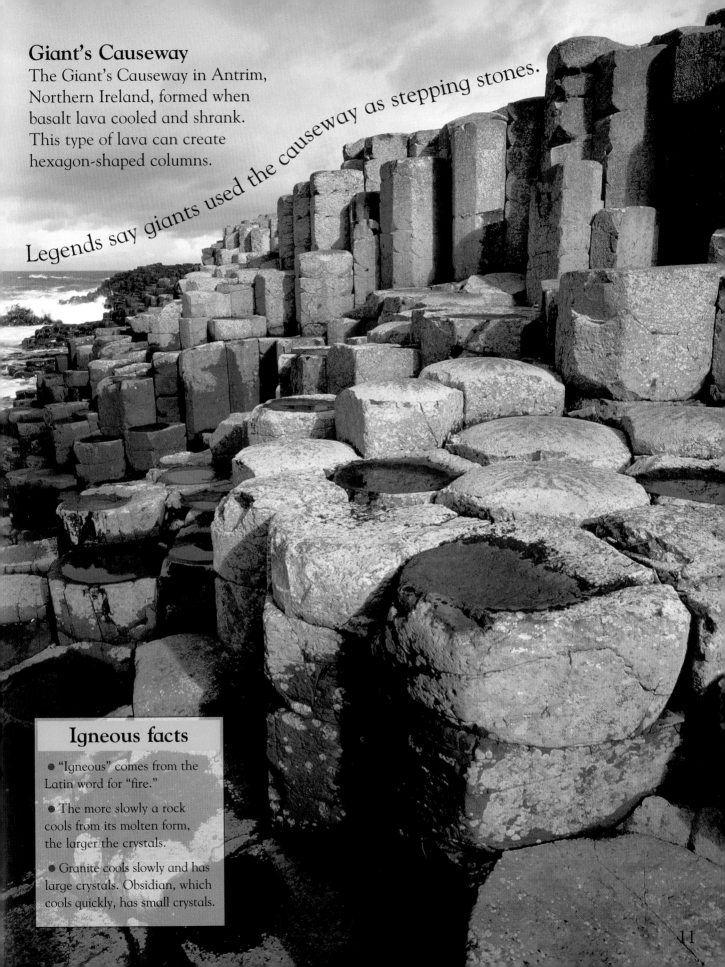

Giant's Causeway

The Giant's Causeway in Antrim, Northern Ireland, formed when basalt lava cooled and shrank. This type of lava can create hexagon-shaped columns.

Legends say giants used the causeway as stepping stones.

Igneous facts

● "Igneous" comes from the Latin word for "fire."

● The more slowly a rock cools from its molten form, the larger the crystals.

● Granite cools slowly and has large crystals. Obsidian, which cools quickly, has small crystals.

11

Sedimentary rock

Towering chalk cliffs are an amazing example of sedimentary rock. They are formed from the shells and skeletons of microscopic sea creatures. Just imagine how many are needed to build a cliff.

In places, these cliffs are 300 ft (90 m) high.

One by one
The sea creatures that break down to create chalk are tiny. It's thought that these cliffs grew by 0.02 in (0.5 mm) a year—that's about 180 of these creatures piled on top of one another.

Movements in Earth's crust have lifted the cliffs out of the sea.

From plant to rock
Another way in which sedimentary rocks form is by the breakdown of plants. As they are buried, they are squeezed together, eventually forming coal.

Year 1...

From plant matter...

to peat...

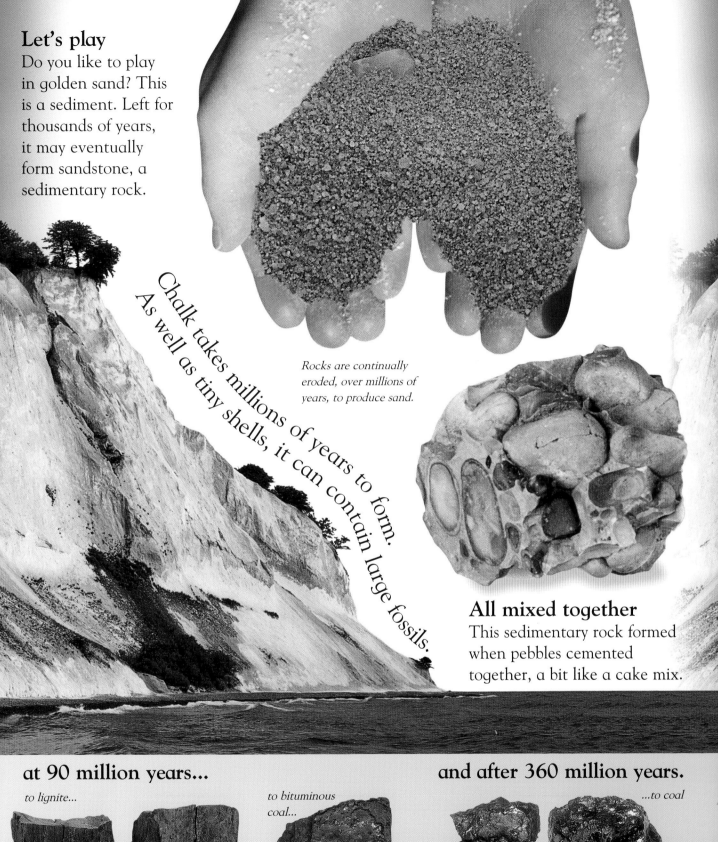

Let's play
Do you like to play in golden sand? This is a sediment. Left for thousands of years, it may eventually form sandstone, a sedimentary rock.

Rocks are continually eroded, over millions of years, to produce sand.

Chalk takes millions of years to form. As well as tiny shells, it can contain large fossils.

All mixed together
This sedimentary rock formed when pebbles cemented together, a bit like a cake mix.

at 90 million years...
to lignite...

and after 360 million years.
...to coal

to bituminous coal...

13

Metamorphic rock

"Metamorphic" comes from the ancient Greek words *meta* (meaning change) and *morphe* (meaning form). When rocks are heated or compressed, this type of rock forms.

Underground changes

One way metamorphic rocks form is when mountains are pushed up out of Earth's crust. Mountains and hills surround this old slate quarry.

A peek at slate

The metamorphic rock slate forms from mud and a rock called shale. The shale has been squeezed and compressed as mountains are pushed up. Slate splits easily into sheets.

Each block weighs thousands of tons.

Marble can be carved into statues.

Marble magic

Marble is a beautiful metamorphic rock. It is mined by being cut into huge blocks with strong cutting wires.

Ice-cream swirls

When rocks are heated, parts may begin to melt and run through a "host" rock. This makes swirly-patterned metamorphic rock. The rock is called migmatite.

A shimmering palace

Polished marble looks stunning when used for building, and perhaps the world's most famous marble building is the Taj Mahal in India. The marble shimmers in the sun.

The dark host rock contains swirls of a lighter-colored rock.

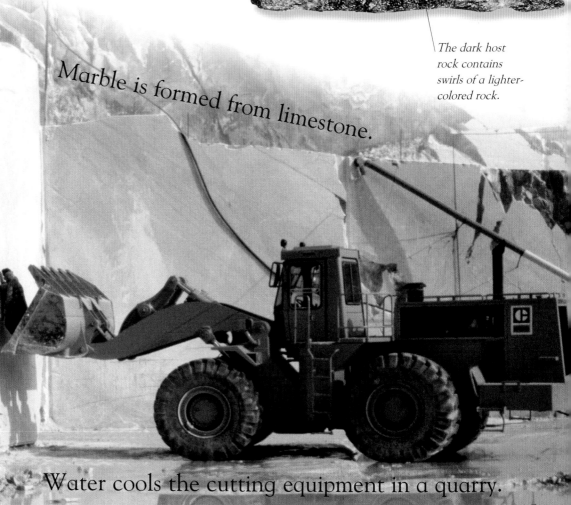

Marble is formed from limestone.

Water cools the cutting equipment in a quarry.

Rocks from space

We cannot see it, but about 25 tons of dust rains down on Earth every day. This fine dust arrives from space. Occasionally a rock from space hits Earth; this is called a meteorite.

A meteorite hit

Meteorites are pieces of rock or metal that hit Earth. Some have broken off asteroids, large chunks of rock that orbit the Sun between Mars and Jupiter. Most are fragments of comets.

There is evidence that a massive meteorite hit Earth 65 million years ago, causing the dinosaurs to die out.

Meteorites hit Earth. Meteors burn up above it. Comets pass on by.

What's inside?

Meteorites from asteroids contain metals such as iron, as well as rocks. Those from comets contain more rock than metal.

The pitted surface is created by the immense heat as the meteor "rubs" against the atmosphere.

Most meteors are the size of a small pebble.

ONCE IN A LIFETIME

One of the most famous comets, Halley's, was included in the Bayeux Tapestry, which was stitched more than 900 years ago. This comet passes Earth just once every 76 years. It last passed us in 1986.

A comet's tail is narrow, but it can stretch for hundreds of miles.

I spy a shooting star

Meteors or shooting stars can be seen as they burn up in Earth's atmosphere, usually more than 50 miles (80 km) above our heads.

Just passing

Comets are a bit like huge snowballs, but made of ice, gases, and dust. They orbit the Sun, developing long tails as they near Earth.

What's that hole?

If a large meteorite hits Earth, it can form a crater, changing the surroundings where it lands. It would take you about 30 minutes to walk across this meteorite crater in Australia.

This crater is so old that trees have grown in its base.

A large meteorite may be traveling at 25,000 mph (40,000 km/h) when it hits.

Hidden beauty

Brrrr! A cave is a damp, dark, chilly place. However, if you are lucky enough to visit a large cave that has been lit and opened to visitors, you'll discover incredibly beautiful shapes in the rocks.

This stream falls farther than the length of a soccer field.

This cave has opened into a vast cavern.

Water damage
Over the course of thousands of years, a constant flow of water will eat away at a solid area of rock. After 100,000 years, this may have formed a small cave, which will continue to grow.

Build it up

Cave formations can be amazingly complicated. These slender shapes have built up gradually, as drops of water deposited traces of a mineral called calcite.

A funny shape

Stalactites hang down while stalagmites grow up. It can take 1,000 years for these formations to grow less than half an inch.

Rock formations in caves build up drip by drip.

These volcanic caves were once mined for millstones.

Soft center

Have you ever eaten a hard candy with a soft center? Volcanic caves can form when soft lava pushes through a hardened outer layer.

The tallest stalagmite in the world is the height of a six-story house.

Breakdown

Rocks are not as permanent as you may think. From driving rain to frothy seas, when rocks are exposed to wind, water, glaciers, or shifts in temperature, changes begin to happen.

The layers that make up the sedimentary rock in these hoodoos can be clearly seen.

Attack by sea

A long time ago, these stacks were a part of Australia's coastline, but they have been cut off from the coast after an ongoing battering from the sea.

The surrounding rock has been washed away.

Attack by wind and water

Hoodoos are columns of soft sandstone topped by harder rock caps. The cap has protected the rock beneath it from being washed away by heavy downpours of rain.

Attack by acid rain

Pollution from cars and trucks attacks rock. The gases are carried in rainwater to make acids that eat into rock—as shown by the damage to this sculpture.

Attack by river

Over millions of years, the Colorado River has carved its way down into the Grand Canyon, exposing rock faces 6,000 ft (1,830 m) deep.

Hoodoos form spectacular shapes, all clustered together.

If a hoodoo loses its protective cap, the structure will soon begin to wear away.

Erosion creates sediment.

Erosion facts

- The wearing away of a landscape is known as erosion.

- Plants add to rock erosion as their roots burrow their way into cracks in rocks.

- When rocks are broken down where they stand, it is known as weathering.

The force of a glacier is enough to crumble rock.

Carving a path

A glacier is a huge mass of slow-moving ice. Born as snow builds up at the top of a mountain, it begins to force its way forward, picking up rocks and boulders as it moves.

Slow progress
Glaciers usually creep just an inch or two each day. They end lower down the mountain, where the water melts away, or at the coast, where large blocks break off.

22

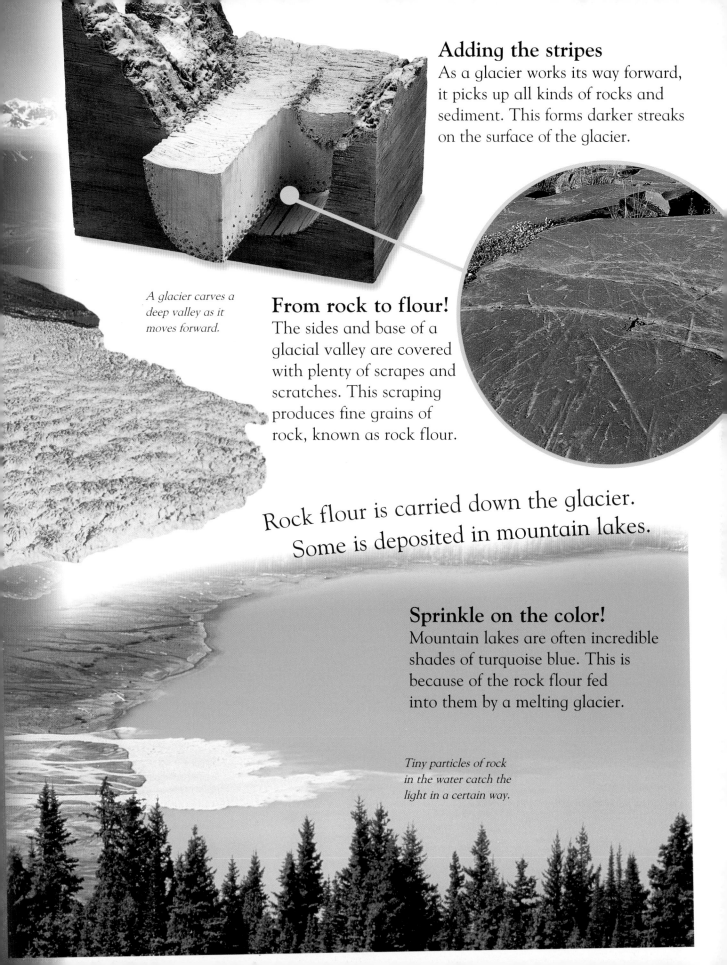

Adding the stripes

As a glacier works its way forward, it picks up all kinds of rocks and sediment. This forms darker streaks on the surface of the glacier.

A glacier carves a deep valley as it moves forward.

From rock to flour!

The sides and base of a glacial valley are covered with plenty of scrapes and scratches. This scraping produces fine grains of rock, known as rock flour.

Rock flour is carried down the glacier. Some is deposited in mountain lakes.

Sprinkle on the color!

Mountain lakes are often incredible shades of turquoise blue. This is because of the rock flour fed into them by a melting glacier.

Tiny particles of rock in the water catch the light in a certain way.

Crystals

Have you ever cut a paper snowflake? Snowflakes are made from small ice crystals that collide and stick together. Crystals also form in rock, and can be cut and polished.

Beautiful colors

Many crystals come in a rich range of colors. This purple amethyst is a form of quartz. It can also be lilac or mauve.

From little to big

The tiny crystals that make up the endless golden sands of a desert are made of quartz. Quartz can also form gigantic crystals. The largest known rock crystal was about 20 ft (6 m) long!

Crystals continue to grow as long as the surrounding conditions remain the same.

ROCKSICLES, ANYONE?

The word crystal comes from the Greek word *kyros*, which means "icy cold." The ancient Greeks thought quartz crystals were made of ice that had frozen so hard it could not melt.

Amethyst is prized for its color.

Is it a thread?

Not all rock crystals are hard. This is a crystal called tremolite. It forms flexible strands similar to the fibers in material. But you wouldn't be able to sew with tremolite. It could make you sick.

Strands of tremolite have a silky, translucent look because light passes through the fibers.

Seems a bit salty

Salt may not seem like a rock, but it is a crystalline rock. In Bolivia there is even a hotel built from salt bricks, including the chairs and tables!

Salt crystals form when seawater evaporates.

The power to heal?

Some people believe that certain crystals have special powers. Jade is thought to help relaxation, lapis lazuli to help friendships.

Lapis lazuli

Polished jade

What a gem!

From sparkling diamonds to rich red rubies, some rocks are valuable and are known as gems. They are mined from the Earth at huge expense, cut and polished, and made into jewelry.

Not just a rock

Most gemstones come from rocks. Just imagine if you were lucky enough to find this rock, with its red rubies.

A gem is a stone that has a beautiful color.

Gemstones such as rubies can be rounded and polished or cut.

Shine on

A cut stone reflects more light, just like this diamond. A cut diamond may have as many as 58 flat sides. Diamond is the hardest mineral of all.

Which are you?

Do you know your birthstone? Some people believe it is lucky to wear a gem that is linked to their month of birth.

January	February	March	April	May
Garnet	*Amethyst*	*Aquamarine*	*Diamond*	*Emerald*

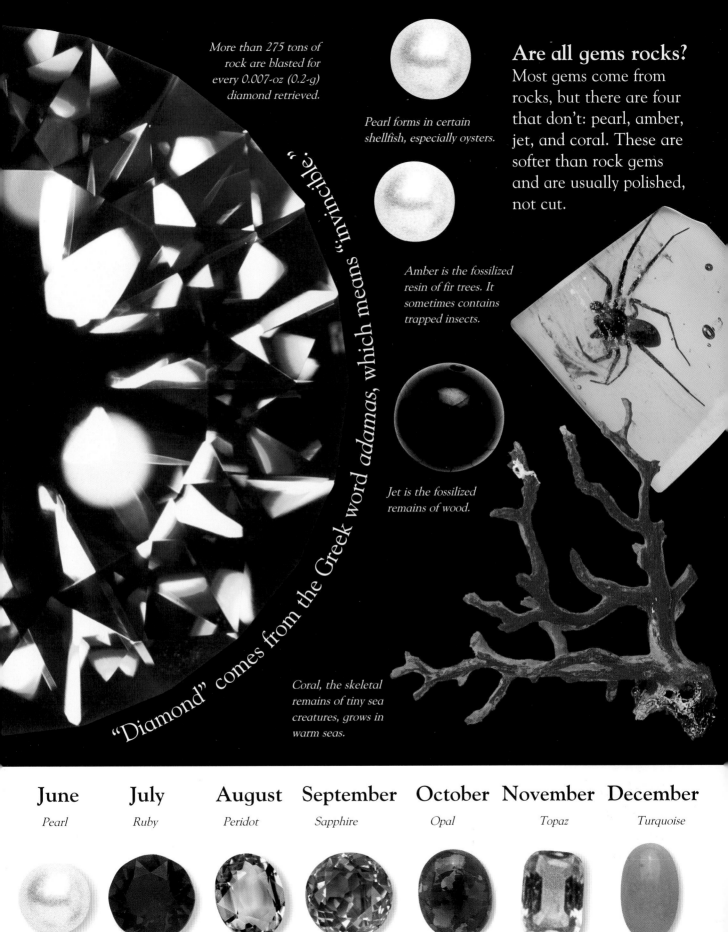

More than 275 tons of rock are blasted for every 0.007-oz (0.2-g) diamond retrieved.

Pearl forms in certain shellfish, especially oysters.

Are all gems rocks?
Most gems come from rocks, but there are four that don't: pearl, amber, jet, and coral. These are softer than rock gems and are usually polished, not cut.

Amber is the fossilized resin of fir trees. It sometimes contains trapped insects.

Jet is the fossilized remains of wood.

"Diamond" comes from the Greek word adamas, which means "invincible."

Coral, the skeletal remains of tiny sea creatures, grows in warm seas.

June	July	August	September	October	November	December
Pearl	Ruby	Peridot	Sapphire	Opal	Topaz	Turquoise

Precious metals

Gems are not the only treasures hidden deep within our rocky planet. Precious metals such as gold, silver, and platinum have long been mined and used to make objects of great beauty.

Gold is sometimes found in veins of quartz.

Gold

Bangkok, Thailand, is home to the Golden Buddha, a religious statue made of solid gold. It weighs 6 tons (5.5 metric tons)—the weight of a small truck.

Platinum

Platinum is the most expensive metal of all. No wonder it was used to make this crown, part of the British Crown Jewels.

This rare platinum nugget weighs the same as 10 apples.

Silver is sometimes found with a delicate frondlike shape.

Silver

Seven hundred years ago, silver was more valuable than gold. This soft metal was used for coins and jewelry—and for statues such as this Hindu figure.

Get that metal!

Some metals are held inside rocks as minerals—the rock that holds the mineral is known as the ore. Some ores are near the surface, some are deep underground.

Copper pipe
Some of the copper extracted from the mine below will be used to make copper pipes.

Boom!
An open-pit mine is a noisy place. The miners constantly blast away at the rock so they can take it away and extract the metal.

Let's make a hole
Most metals are collected from open-pit mines. This means that the surface is blasted and tons of rock are removed, truckload by truckload.

Mix them together...

Metals are often melted down and mixed with other metals to make a stronger metal—an alloy.

An open-pit mine has a network of roads.

...to get

When copper and tin are mixed together, they produce bronze, which can be used to make casts.

Copper ore

Tin ore

Bronze casts are made by pouring molten metal into a mold. It then sets.

A GIFT FROM SPACE

Not all metals come from the ground. Six thousand years ago, many people knew iron as "the metal from the sky," probably because the first iron that people used came from meteorites.

31

Using rocks in art

Have you ever used a rock to draw? It's great fun to use chalk and scribble away on a sidewalk. The colors held inside some rocks and minerals have been used by artists for thousands of years.

Who needs paper?
Cave painters had no paper, so they used rock as their canvas. They used a mixture of materials to produce just four or five colors.

Cave paintings date back 20,000 years.

Cave painters used charcoal—the remains of burned wood—to make black.

Chalk was used by the ancient Romans to lighten the face.

A light source

The sedimentary rock chalk is messy to use, but it is a fantastic material to use to show how light bounces off an object.

Arty facts

● Chalk was used to make the first white coloring for art.

● Clay was often used by early artists as a coloring for green and brown.

● For thousands of years, people crushed colored rocks and mixed the powder with animal fat to make paints.

Gold was extracted from a mineral and used in this 600-year-old painting.

Cinnabar was first used in ancient China.

Rich reds

The powder of a mineral rock called cinnabar makes a brilliant red that was widely used in religious art in the Middle Ages.

Cinnabar is the main source of the poisonous metal mercury.

Rocks in history

A long time ago, somebody somewhere picked up a stone and used it as a tool. It was the beginning of something big, as people found more and more ways in which to use rocks.

Just down the road

In the past, there were no machines to move building materials, so people had to use what was available nearby. These roofs are covered with slate taken from a local quarry.

A helpful handle

Hand-held rocks were gradually combined with handles to make axes. This stone was held in a length of wood by a tightly bound length of twine.

The handle has been remade— the original rotted away long ago.

It takes a long time to hand-grind the grain for a loaf of bread.

Let's make flour

Grain was first ground to make flour in this way some 6,000 years ago. Rocks like these were an early tool for crushing the grain, but they made a coarse flour.

Flint scraper

Flint has sharp edges and was widely used in prehistory. The first flint tools, like this fur scraper, were basic—but did the job.

Lift, scrape, and clean the fur.

Taking shape

Flint can be shaped by chipping at it with another stone. That's how this 4,500-year-old arrowhead was made.

Building rocks

Take a look around you. Rocks are everywhere—in the sidewalks and the roads, in the houses in which we live, and in the skyscrapers that tower above us. They are the building blocks of modern cities.

From a mold

Bricks are made from clay, which is shaped in molds and fired in huge ovens, called kilns, to bake it.

Skyscrapers

Skyscrapers are built from a variety of manufactured materials on a steel framework. Many of these materials come from rocks that have been mined.

The building's steel framework is strong but also flexible in high winds.

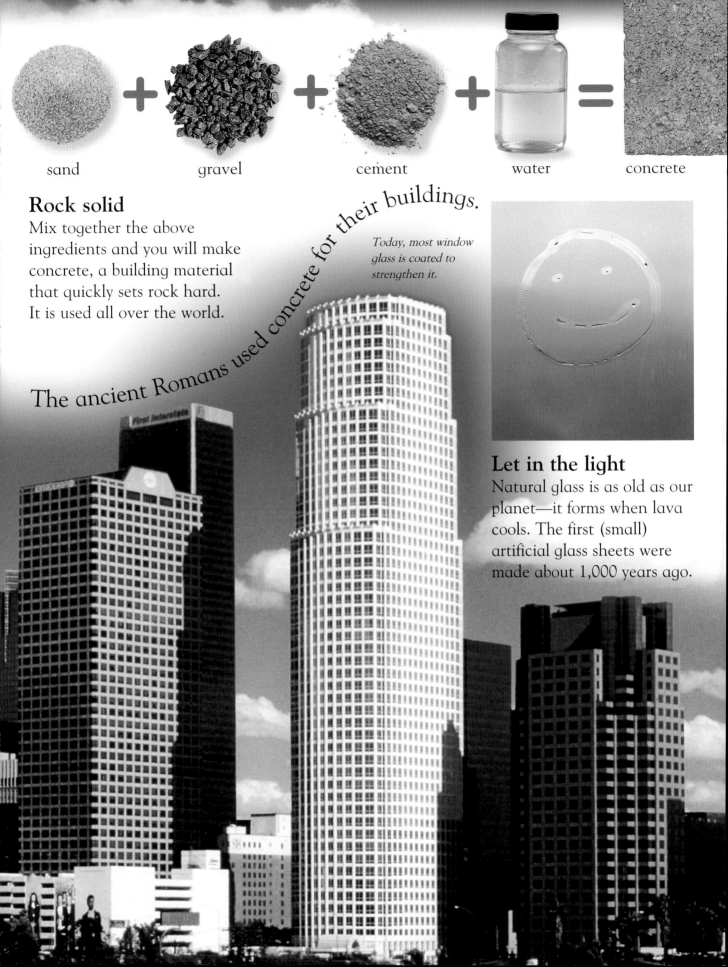

sand + gravel + cement + water = concrete

Rock solid

Mix together the above ingredients and you will make concrete, a building material that quickly sets rock hard. It is used all over the world.

The ancient Romans used concrete for their buildings.

Today, most window glass is coated to strengthen it.

Let in the light

Natural glass is as old as our planet—it forms when lava cools. The first (small) artificial glass sheets were made about 1,000 years ago.

A touch of mystery

Some rocks and minerals look so
unusual that myths and legends
have grown up around them.
From Devil's toenails to
desert roses, the weird
and wonderful are
all around us.

*Wave Rock is
the height of a
three-story house.*

A HISSING STONE?

Snakestones were once believed to be the
remains of coiled snakes turned to
stone by a 7th-century abbess
called St. Hilda. They are
actually ammonites, the
fossils of shelled sea creatures,
which were sometimes given
carved snake heads.

Surf's up

Wave Rock in Australia is well named. This
massive rock is one-and-a-half times the
length of a jumbo jet. It has formed as much
softer rock beneath the upper lip wears away.

Taking root

Is it a tree root, or maybe an animal's burrow? No. This is fulgurite. It forms when lightning strikes sand and fuses the grains.

The forks follow the lightning's path.

Are they toenail clippings?

These rocks were once believed to be the Devil's toenails. In fact, they are fossils—the remains of oyster shells.

Fulgurite is a glassy rock.

Which way?

Magnetite is a magnetic mineral and was used in early compasses. We now use magnetite to produce iron—it contains a lot of iron.

Is it real?

Desert roses look very pretty, but they have no smell. They form in the desert from a mineral called barite.

The streaks are caused by minerals being washed down the rock by downpours of rain.

History in a rock

Rocks hide a lot of things, but perhaps the most exciting are the secrets rocks tell about life on Earth millions of years ago, when the dinosaurs ruled.

A dead beginning

A dinosaur lies down to die on a sandy shore. Perhaps it will not be eaten, and its skeleton will remain intact as its flesh rots away. The long path to becoming a fossil has begun.

A special scientist called a paleontologist can discover how old a fossil is by

What's that?

Imagine your footsteps being found by somebody in the future, preserved forever in rock. Fossil footprints are a curious reminder of creatures long dead.

The fossils that have been discovered are only a tiny percentage of the animals that have lived.

Fossil dinosaur

The skeleton of this dinosaur has been preserved because the animal was covered in mud soon after death and squeezed between layers of sediment.

studying the rocks around it.

Big gnashers

Teeth are one of the most commonly found fossils—they last well because they are so hard. These belonged to a dinosaur called Iguanodon.

Clean up time

It takes a long time to extract a large fossil from the rock in which it is encased. The paleontologist working on it does not want to damage it.

This is the fossilized skeleton of a meat-eating dinosaur called Gasosaurus.

The rock and dust surrounding a fossil are removed particle by particle if necessary.

Fossil facts

● The parts of an animal most likely to fossilize are the hard bits: the bones, teeth, or shell.

● Fossils of footprints, or trackways, are called trace fossils.

● Fossils are found in sedimentary rock, such as limestone.

Hunting for rocks

Once you begin to learn about rocks and minerals, it's fun to go and look for some interesting rocks yourself. You may find a rock containing a fossil!

The spiral pattern of this long-fossilized ammonite can be seen in the nautilus shells of today.

Leave no stone unturned

This child is looking for fossils. Depending on where in the world you live, you may have to be careful when looking for rocks: in some countries they hide dangerous creatures.

Start your rock collection by hunting for pebbles of different colors.

Mohs scale

Geologists use the Mohs scale, which was set up in 1812, to measure a rock's hardness. The higher the number, the harder the rock.

1	2	2.5 fingernail	3	4
Talc	Gypsum		Calcite	Fluorite

The nautilus builds its shell from calcium.

Comparing a live horseshoe crab with a fossilized one shows how little the animal has changed.

Just like today

Some fossils resemble animals that are alive today. This section of a nautilus shell shows the chambers that were also found in ancient ammonites.

Still going strong

"Living fossils" are creatures that were known as fossils before living examples were found. Horseshoe crabs are living fossils.

Pass another potato!

You may be lucky enough to find one of these. It's called a potato rock. From the outside it looks a little bit like a moldy old potato. This hides a beautiful interior.

5	**5.5**	**6**	**7**	**8**	**9**	**10**
Apatite	**Steel nail**	**Orthoclase**	**Quartz**	**Topaz**	**Corundum**	**Diamond**

43

What does it make?

Rocks and minerals, and the metals that are taken from them, can be found in many of the everyday objects that surround you. Just take a look!

Clay is used in...
books
pencils
pottery

Fluorite is used in...
toothpaste
ceramics
water

Garnet is used in...
sandpaper
glass
jewelry

Limestone is used in...
cleaning products
books
concrete

Quartz is used in...

computers

radios

watch batteries

Silica sand is used in...

televisions

glass

plastic buckets

Silver is used in...

telephones

cameras

picture frames

Sulfur is used in...

film

matches

paper

45

Talc is used in...

paint

ceramics

talcum powder

45

Glossary

Here are the meanings of some words it is useful to know
when learning about rocks and minerals.

Alloy a metal that is made by combining two or more metals.

Basalt one of the most common forms of igneous rock.

Coal a rock made from plants that have been buried and squeezed over millions of years.

Crystal a naturally occurring substance with a specific makeup that forms particular types of minerals.

Erosion the wearing away of a landscape.

Fossil the preserved remains of ancient life or evidence of their activity.

Glacier a mass of ice or snow that flows under its own weight.

Igneous rock rock made from molten rock that has cooled and hardened.

Hoodoo a column of soft rock with a harder lid, which protects it from erosion.

Lava the molten rock (magma) that has erupted from a volcano.

Lignite a woody kind of rock made from plants before they become coal.

Magma molten rock found deep inside the Earth.

Mantle the part of the Earth's interior that lies between the crust and the core.

Metamorphic rock rock melted by heat and pressure that cools and recrystallizes in a different form.

Meteor a lump of rock or metal from outer space that burns up as it enters Earth's atmosphere.

Meteorite a meteor that has fallen to Earth.

Mineral a naturally occurring substance with very specific characteristics, such as hardness.

Nugget a small piece of something valuable, like gold.

Open-pit mine a mine with an open top, instead of tunnels under Earth's surface.

Ore a rock that holds minerals.

Quarry a place where stone is dug up.

Sediment pieces of rock, and plant and animal material, that are carried by water, wind, or ice and usually deposited some way from their origin.

Sedimentary rock rock that is formed when small pieces of rock or plant and animal remains become stuck together.

Weathering the breakdown of rock by the weather.

Index

Acknowledgments

Dorling Kindersley would like to thank:
Dorian Spencer Davies for original artwork, and Fleur Star for help with the glossary.

Picture credits

The publisher would like to thank the following for their kind permission to reproduce their photographs: (Abbreviations key: t=top, b=bottom, r=right, l=left, c=center; DK:NHM=DK Picture Library: Natural History Museum, SPL= Science Photo Library)

1 Corbis: David Forman/Eye Ubiquitous; 2-3 Corbis: Darrell Gulin; 5tr & tcr DK:NHM, 5bl & bcl GeoScience Features Picture Library, 5bcr Corbis: Lester V Bergman, 6t Getty Images: Schafer & Hill, 7tl SPL: Stephen & Donna O'Meara, 8bl Corbis: James A.Sugar, 8-9c Getty Images: Spencer Jones, 8-9b SPL: Bill Bachman, 9t Corbis: Galen Rowell, 9tl & cl DK:NHM, 9c & b Corbis: M. Angelo, 10bl Corbis: Martin Jones, 10br GeoScience Features Picture Library, 11 Corbis: Ric Ergenbright, 11tcr DK:NHM, 12-13 Ardea London Ltd: Ake Lindau, 12c Ardea London Ltd: P.Morris, 12 bl & br DK:NHM, 13c, bl, bc & br DK:NHM, 13t Powerstock: Liane Cary, 14-15 Corbis: WildCountry, 14tl Corbis: Richard Klune, 14tr GeoScience Features Picture Library, 14b Corbis: Araldode Luca, 16-17 SPL: Mike Agliolo,

16r SPL: Detlev Van Ravenswaay, 17c SPL: Eckhard Slawik,17t SPL: Mehau Kulyk, 17b SPL: Bill Bachman, 18 Corbis: Annie Griffiths Belt, 18tl DK:NHM, 19t Corbis: Craig Lovell, 19b Corbis: Roger Ressmeyer, 20-21 SPL: David Nunuk, 20r Corbis: Royalty-Free, 22-23 SPL: Bernhard Edmaier, 22t SPL: Simon Fraser, 23c Ardea London Ltd: Francois Gohier, 24 SPL: Sinclair Stammers, 25t DK:NHM, 25cr SPL: Cristina Pedrazzini, 25 bl & br SPL: Vaughan Fleming, 26-27 & 26bcr SPL: Alfred Pasieka, 26tl SPL: J.C.Revy, 26c SPL: Lawrence Lawry, 26bl DK:NHM, 27tr, crb, br, bcr & brl DK:NHM, 28-29 Corbis: Lindsay Hebberd, 28l Corbis: ML Sinibaldi, 29r Corbis: Tim Graham, 30-31 Corbis: Yann Arthus-Bertrand, 30b Getty Images: Jaime Villaseca, 31tl DK:NHM, 31b Corbis: The State Russian Museum, 32 Corbis Sygma: Pierre Vauthey, 33tr DK Picture Library: Museo de Zaragoza, 33c DK Picture Library: Museum of London, 33bl Corbis: David Lees, 34 Corbis: Ric Ergenbright, 35tr & bl DK Picture Library: Museum of London, 35br DK Picture Library: British Museum, 36-37 Corbis: Lee White, 37tl DK:NHM, 37cb Corbis: Michael Prince, 38-39 Ardea London Ltd: Jean-Paul Ferrero, 39tl SPL: Astrid & Hanns-Frieder, 39tr SPL: Peter Menzel, 39cl DK:NHM, 39br SPL: Martin Land, 40-41 SPL: Mehau Kulyk, 40tl DK:NHM, 40bc SPL: Sinclair Stammers, 42-43 SPL: Lawrence Lawry, 42cl Getty Images: Clarissa Leahy, Corbis: Jeffrey L. Rotman, 43bcl DK:NHM, 43br SPL: Alfred Pasieka, 44tr DK Picture Library: British Museum, 45tl DK:NHM, 46-47 Corbis: Owaki-Kulla, 48l & 49r SPL: Dr. Jeremy Burgess.

All other images © Dorling Kindersley.
For further information see: www.dkimages.com